LOSING ITHACA

LOSING ITHACA

CHRISTOPHER SOUTHGATE

Shoestring Press

All rights reserved. No part of this work covered by the copyright herein may be reproduced or used in any means – graphic, electronic, or mechanical, including copying, recording, taping, or information storage and retrieval systems – without written permission of the publisher.

Printed by imprintdigital
Upton Pyne, Exeter
www.digital.imprint.co.uk

Typesetting and cover design by The Book Typesetters
hello@thebooktypesetters.com
07422 598 168
www.thebooktypesetters.com

Published by Shoestring Press
19 Devonshire Avenue, Beeston, Nottingham, NG9 1BS
(0115) 925 1827
www.shoestringpress.co.uk

First published 2023
© Copyright: Christopher Southgate
© Cover photograph: Frankie Fraser

The moral right of the author has been asserted.

ISBN 978-1-915553-25-6

ACKNOWLEDGEMENTS

'Notes from a ditch near Troy' was short-listed for the 2022 Bridport Prize.

Versions of some of these poems have appeared in *Allegro, Frogmore Papers, Orbis, Pratik, Raceme,* and *The Temenos Review.* Five poems from Section III appeared in the March/April 2023 issue of the journal *Theology.*

I thank the many poets who have given me feedback over the last few years, and especially my publisher John Lucas for his sustained encouragement and critical attention, which has been a particular benefit in finalising this collection.

I also thank very particularly all those friends who have helped me through recent difficult times, especially two groups at our local church whose kindness and always care-ful support have been such a source of comfort and affirmation.

For my dearest Sandy, my love in sorrow and in joy

CONTENTS

I
Notes from a ditch near Troy	3
Farewell to Stromness	4
Facts of Farewell	5
London St Pancras International	6
Grief music	8
Rose-petals	9
Year Five	10

II
Six reasons why I am in love with Greta Thunberg	13
Six New Year's Resolutions	14
Six reasons why I will never throw away my mother's address book	15
Six Ingredients of Self-Care	16
Six sixes in an over	17
And on the sixth day?	18

III
Three Versions of Judas	21
Did Jesus hear birdsong	22
Woman behold thy son	23
Altarpiece, St Mary-le-Bow	25
The takes at Emmaus	26
Thorn in the flesh	27
Etty Hillesum 1914–43	28
Matisse and God: a prayer	29

IV
Malignant Sadness	33
Accompanying Malignant Sadness	34
December jay	35

Pastoral encouragement from the latest exoplanet research	36
Goldfinches	37
Swifts	38

V

Lexicon	41
Freshman	42
Antonia	43
Scratches	44
A poem of love and envy	45
Seen on a t-shirt	46
The Pearl Earring	48
Keats's Star	49
Hopkins on Symi	50

VI

Eulogy at the memorial service for a glacier	55
Debate on a pandemic	56
'The Fighting Temeraire, tugged to her last berth to be broken up, 1838'	58
Two studies from T.S. Eliot's 'Journey of the Magi'	
Self-appraisal of a mage	59
Such a long journey	60
Bowling Green Marsh, Topsham	61
Deer, toward dusk	62
Better Worlds	63
Rabbit Hole	64
Ladies who trek	65
Parthenon in sunlight, gateway in shadow	66
Petroglyphs, Arizona	67
A Place for Poetry	68

I

NOTES FROM A DITCH NEAR TROY

After such a death we should sit on the ground
Tearing our clothes and throwing dust on our heads.
We put on suits and unaccustomed ties
Ushered about by professionals in practised solemnity.

Women are allowed to weep, and do,
Tugging at little-worn business skirts,
Unearthing family handkerchiefs.

Men are stiff, because this is proper,
And because we take our cue from the husband
Who manages to do stiffness
With a certain greatness of spirit

He found in his wife. It is the music
That so utterly undermines us. It holds,
Between one note and the next, all anguish.

While it plays we are Priam
Bearing away ransomed Hector, and lovely
Andromache tasting emptiness,
Future absent all joy.

When we shuffle out we are ourselves,
Each with our own dust in our hair,
Each wrapped in a torn scarf of memory.

FAREWELL TO STROMNESS

I reconstruct the last fortnight of your life.
As you sit at your piano the days are full of sunshine –
light touches gracefully the lines
of your loved face. For you are loved
and more even than you can know,
so many fill the crem for your funeral,
endure the space of quiet in an Orcadian lament.

You pick out its slow notes, they gather as they rise.
They have a clarity to them, as of an Orkney harbour
at dawn. You are assembling
the cadences of your requiem.

Gradually more fluent as your fingers unstiffen
as they bridge more and more surely
the big chords, transition
into the high repeated counter-theme
and back – I see you smile then
as the logic of the piece reasserts.

There are farewells – they come sooner
than anyone dreamed. You are loved
reasonably and beyond all reason.
I am eating mango with a twist of lime
in other sunlight far away, when on the phone
they tell me you are dead –
                                    after a year this still
seems less real than you at your piano-stool
loved and finally at peace with yourself
assembling your requiem.

The title is the title of a piece for solo piano by Peter Maxwell Davies.

FACTS OF FAREWELL

Last leavetakings are simple –
Sung with a lift on an ever-dying fall.
Afterward the facts
Taste faintly of yearning.

Never again to hear the half-laugh in your greeting
Which once I took for mockery.
Never the slight quaver in your voice
As we go deeper, into love or myth.

Of course, there will be no more of the mistakes
When I fail to tune to your mood.
But even the mistunings
I know that I shall long for.

Of course, it is up to me
To read in the flash of light on slate-grey sea
Recollection of your eyes
At moments of delight.

Of course, it is up to me
To keep believing, and find words
For memories
And make the words dance again.

However enduring the shape of loved hills
However beautiful the shawls of evening
However skilful the rituals of parting
However well-judged the last, precious hug,

The facts of farewell
Taste mainly of yearning.

LONDON ST PANCRAS INTERNATIONAL

A young man plays Joplin's 'Entertainer'
on the concourse piano.
> *There is no poetry in my heart, only wistfulness*
> *for a gathering that never happened.*

The world goes by with its backpack, oblivious.
The concourse paces out life. A little girl
whose shoes light up to match her bright pink bag
dances along on her child-rein.
The piano player attracts the inevitable camera-phones
> *I capture the thought*
> that always we must capture rather than pay attention.

Now another young man sits at the piano, sets down twelve red
roses, plays jazz.
With his left foot crossed behind the pedal foot
and his grey cap at its exact angle
he is the epitome of cool. Yet the roses speak risk.
Two girls, sisters, practise their dance moves to his beat
> *I decide the roses are pretty safe. But who am I to know?*
> *I was sure the five of us, constellated around our shared love of you,*
> *would meet in this place and mix and match*
> *and argue about Impressionism*
> *and make up on the Ile St Louis.*
> Impossibly you are gone. Four years
> do not make this less impossible.

A grey-headed man is at the piano now,
riffing on Elton John. 'How wonderful life is..'
> *How bizarre life is, that I am here*
> *to write lines to time*
> *and your song is not heard*
> *in this depleted world.*

The young man clutches his bouquet moodily
his princess, or prince, must be late, or a no-show.
She comes, he delivers the roses, takes her hand.

They wander together into the London night
        their fairy-tale extended.

But now this is real life, because high-vis jackets emerge
                                    to place signs
by the piano, welcoming arrivals from Ukraine,
traumas compressed into suitcases.
    How wonderful life is
that love was, and is not forgotten.
      How wonderful life is
        while it can be watched in safety.

GRIEF MUSIC

At first it thundered through everything.
It was the Great Gate of Kiev
grand, unbearable, insistent, wistful.

Then all I was left with
was a set of reverberations
stretching space, always dying away

and the black of the Steinway
as black-clad intermediaries
shut down its lid.

Then it was a set of roaming dissonances
searching sound-palettes late at night, revealing always
the sheer wrongness of things.

I would like to get to a place of balance
where I could imagine us
listening to the same waterfall.

And yes, undertones would come and go,
never clutched at. Bells of memory might ring anger or failure,
quiet, floating joy.

If only two successive violin-chords
crossed falling water at the same pitch
then I would be healed.

ROSE-PETALS

For my mother's wedding
my grandmother picked all the petals
off her roses, for friends to scatter on the couple.

She threw beauty at her loss.
Late in life she planted old roses
in a brick-paved sun-trap. As the bricks warmed

rose-scent filled the air.

Fifty years on
I plant roses wherever I can
searching, searching for that flood of gift.

I catch it only
in faint drifts. Last night it rained hard
battering from my new roses

every last petal.

YEAR FIVE

What is the reminder of grief like?
Like losing one's footing on a crag
and being swept down a waterfall.
The footholds are lost in a second
but the falling seems slow, slow,
the wounding not mortal but deep, deep.

And one can run simulations –
step into falling – re-evoke the pain
to deaden it by over-use.
I have found inoculation
ineffective
     try as I might
I cannot get at the hurt

that comes to me on shafts of sunlight
in places you would have been
things you would have said.
We keep company only in the falling,
reminders of the wounding
and I want that togetherness

that traces a track, always different
down and down. No new words
come. You never smile. I feel
you show me that you know
you are not forgotten. That is all.
I return to climbing the crag.
The holds are loose, fracturing,
                        I climb.

II

SIX REASONS WHY I AM IN LOVE WITH GRETA THUNBERG

One. The first time ever I saw her face
She was sitting in a crumpled yellow raincoat
Having a royal sulk outside her school gates.

Two. When President Trump passed by in his pomp,
Full entourage around him, after his fourteen minutes
At the climate summit, her face was pure disdain.

Three. When he tweeted that she needed
Help with anger management, she tweeted back
That she was indeed receiving this.

Four. This is her century. She may live to see it out.
And I who would be glad to see out this new decade
Want the world to dare to hear her.

Five. My six great-nephews and nieces are relying on her
And I love their bright and wondering eyes
And their passionate playful hearts.

Six. Because the little catches in her Swedish accent
Remind me of Jutte, our au pair when I was nine
And fell in love for the very first time.

SIX NEW YEAR'S RESOLUTIONS

to build more castles in the air

to leave more stones unturned

to see and not believe

to believe without seeing

to find good in the illest of winds

to ponder more deeply the sleeping of cats.

SIX REASONS WHY I WILL NEVER THROW AWAY MY MOTHER'S ADDRESS BOOK

The texture of that old brown leather
stamped with gold round the edges, stained scuffed
survivor of many suitcases.

Random notes she has made – how on earth
to get to a Scottish shooting lodge by train;
a job my father should apply for,
closing date August 1953.
The name of a riding school for my sister.

People and places I have never even heard of.
Reverend Mother Abbess. The Honourable Sir Fenton.
The Coningsby Club. The Astor Hotel.

Because of all the ways she kept track of lives
across the world. Organised and anchored
erratic projects in husband and children.
All the while conducting her own adventures
deep in her imagination.

Because it starts in hope, with her new married name,
her wedding date, their first address –
sans children, sans heartbreak.

And because Heraclitus was right that networks
flourish and fade, last less long
than good leather. And wrong, I am certain – *all* cannot be flux –
the person she was, the hope, the passionate
internal journey, somewhere, surely, persists.

SIX INGREDIENTS OF SELF-CARE

It is said
Everyone should have
Six people in their lives
To whom
They could confide anything.
I had six.

Two have gone missing
I had not dreamed
The gap
They would leave.

SIX SIXES IN AN OVER

On August 31st, 1968, playing for Nottinghamshire against Glamorgan at Sophia Gardens, Cardiff, Garfield Sobers hit the left-arm spin of Malcolm Nash for six sixes in an over.

OK, it wasn't the largest county ground. All right, Notts were way ahead. Granted, Malcolm Nash was no Hedley Verity (no Garry Sobers either) even so, it had never been done.

It reminds me of the time I was due to captain a cricket team against an excessively arrogant guy (why must outrageous talent go home so docilely with odious arrogance?).

Anyway, rain ruined the match. We stood on the boundary in the drizzle. Mr Arrogant borrowed a seven-iron and hit golf balls perfectly, soaring, each one precisely the width of the field.

So the effortless, high-backlift huge-follow-through striking of Sobers that day. Nash was bowling his best stuff. Sobers hit each one like a stationary ball (I'm told he played golf with the same swing).

The smile on his face broadened with each shot, gloriously free of the dull hassle of captaining a declining Test team. And the crowd woke up, stretched, focussed, longed for every shot to clear the rope.

OK, the fifth blow was caught by Roger Davis who fell over the boundary. All right, an easy match on a small ground. But this was music of no common sort. It was talent,

for once, co-habiting with the innocence of true greatness.

AND ON THE SIXTH DAY?

He was, on the whole, pleased with the trees
(gingko was a particular favourite)
and the moon, waning so exquisitely
to a thin blade. And the Pleiades.

A day of creation left. What more could be done?
Perhaps something on the land,
moving across ground with the power and grace
with which orca
        surge through water?
                Or with the focussed intensity
of the peregrine in stoop?

He had it! The Lord God created cheetah, and (of necessity)
young zebra, and antelope of every kind, hurtling
across the savannah in the desperate poetry of escape.

But (and this was perhaps a weakness in the Lord God)
he craved also audience, creatures to watch
spellbound at all this splendour.

So the Lord God made
a slow, slouching, wide-eyed creature
cleverer than all the wild beasts –
a fashioner of masterpieces.

The creature made love,
        stole fire,
             altered air,
lynched his fellows from the trees of the Lord God

and on the seventh day
God hung there, wondering.

III

THREE VERSIONS OF JUDAS

He had heard the talk and the plotting
    He idolised the Master
        He envied all those others
He had begun to have a recurring dream
    He saw him as the true Son of God
        Those the Saviour rescued were trash
In the dream the swat team came for the Lord in the night
    The Christ, the One all Israel longed for
        He had waited patiently
In the dream jackboots were loud on the stair
    The kiss was rescue
        He had balanced the bloody books long enough
No escape from the Temple police
    It was time for the flaming-sword angels
        Enough of foot-anointing whores
The kiss would be the way, and a nice little earner
    This would be his God-given role, for which he would
                        always be remembered
        Enough of flawed, dependent Peter. One last
                        moment, one last kiss.

DID JESUS HEAR BIRDSONG

on the last morning of his life?
Were there sparrows disputing in the dirt
outside the High Priest's house?
Did Mrs Pilate's captive goldfinch
reach him across the courtyard
while the Empire washed its hands?

Did he who had seen beauty in every suffering face
glimpse loveliness anywhere on that climb
to the Place of the Skull?
Did the sun shine on a young girl's jet-black hair?
Did he see pity, in the milky cataracts
of an old beggar's eyes?

Every dragged step of that last climb
was being alive. Did his gaze hunt for faces
that offered something beyond cruelty?
How long could he tune his heart
to the song of the trapped, the silenced
before the only music he knew

beyond the jeering crows
was the cry in his own throat
eloi, eloi, lema sabachthani?

WOMAN BEHOLD THY SON

We sat on the dust of the ground
holding one another. He had given us
to each other, and we were both
holding that, as we watched every breath
rasp out, each one weaker
than the last.

        We willed every breath
to come, as you might will
a sick newborn to breathe, breathe.
Why did we want those breaths,
torn from him when he had already
gasped out that it was finished?

        We could not bear
to begin that time without him, the time
inevitable from the moment of a kiss
under old olive trees. So we
sat in the dust and held
son his new mother, mother a son

        while the light
of our lives wracked out breaths
more blood than air now
till the great wise head
I had held so often in my arms
finally fell.

No tears would come
then, though we had tasted enough
of each other's tears
waiting for the end.
Guards broke the legs of the two thieves
with some sort of crowbar.

I wanted my child in my arms.
First I had to watch a savage spear
enter his dear dead lung. Then a soldier
knocked away the supports, and sent
his cross crashing down. Take
the carcass away, he shouted. Carcass…

My boy, my wise, foolish boy
in my arms at last, while the man
he had loved bathed ravaged
hands and feet. We were so close
in that time, and I could have died
gladly then, before they moved us on,

others appearing as if from nowhere
to carry the body of the Lord
they had abandoned. The two of us
looked at each other, agreed
wordlessly to wait there, writing his name
over and over again

in the dust of the ground.

ALTARPIECE, ST MARY-LE-BOW

The head is completely hollowed out.
The body too is empty –
half-wrapped in beaten steel.

What populates the black inner space
is the polished size of the nails.
One spearing delicate feet, dancer's feet,
one each notional hand.

Death has so hollowed out
this nailed body, there is no flesh
to take down and bury.

There is only speared spirit
passive for the life of the world.
How is it then that the emptiness
compels more than the nails?

THE TAKES AT EMMAUS

It's basically a three-hander, and my plan is to film it
in three episodes, or what I call phases.
One: all cloaks and dusty road,
sadness and shadow. Hopes dashed.
I'll use the hand-held here,
walking backward, and focus on Cleopas
(they want Colin Firth for him –
good at that hang-dog Weltschmerz,
though that rules out Hugh Grant for Christ,
bad undertones of Bridget Jones).
Anyway, long hand-helds for their walking grief,
soft violins keening in the background.

The second I see as hardest.
Let's face it, Bible study is not the stuff
of good cinema. But there could be possibilities –
Sinai, Sea of Reeds, Calvary –
almost like a lecture over a powerpoint
but the voice tasting of sheer sunlight.

And the scene at the inn – tremendous.
I won't show his face directly, only ever
mirrored in the surface of the wine.
Here I can do better than the scriptwriter, fading to and fro
between the Last Supper, that crowd of faces
falling into fear, and my two
in astonished transition out of grief.
Then closeup on the bread, last touched in the face of death –
hard, just for a moment, to stretch out his hand for it.
I won't show the vanishing – no cheap tricks for me –
just the unquestioning surface of the wine,
the bread parted – laid out in blessing.

THORN IN THE FLESH

Of course we don't know. We may guess
at the teacher's attentiveness, the beloved
pupil's response. We may wonder
why Timothy is always being sent away.

We might imagine, how landing
at a certain cove, resting together
on the warm sand, by water so clear
they could watch every octopus
bury itself under rocks, every fish
flash silver, the young man rose
to stare up at the pagan temple
on the hill, and Paul watched
young muscles flex under the taut sun.

At such moments, and in his memory of them,
the thorn burned fierce, as though new-twisted
by the most skilled of tormentors.
He sometimes remembered to pray.

Prayer sometimes made the burning less.

ETTY HILLESUM 1914–43

We must be simple and wordless as the falling rain,
Etty wrote from a space deep inside her.
She threw last postcards out of the Auschwitz train.

*The Lord is my high tower. He remains
Passionately mine, through all the misery and fear.
We must be simple and wordless as the falling rain.*

*We left the camp singing, calm, sustained,
Father and Mother and I, even Mischa.*
She threw last postcards out of the Auschwitz train.

I am sitting on my rucksack (her relentless brain
Always writing, writing, puzzling out adventures)
We must be simple and wordless as the falling rain.

Sitting with the smell of cattle and urine.
Sitting with thoughts of Han, and her other lovers,
Throwing last postcards out of the Auschwitz train.

One more card was found. Mother, in different vein.
'Now nothing will help us any more.' The last we have of her.
We must be simple and wordless as the falling rain
And the high-tower postcard, thrown from the Auschwitz train.

In September 1943 Etty Hillesum, a young Jewish intellectual, was sent from the transit camp at Westerbork, Holland, to Auschwitz, where she died. Her remarkable diaries and letters from the last two years of her short life show a great appreciation of the 'glory' of life, and a remarkable refusal to hate her oppressors. The words in italics are quoted or paraphrased from her writing.

MATISSE AND GOD: A PRAYER

"I don't know whether I believe in God or not. I think, really, I'm some kind of a Buddhist. But the essential thing is to put oneself in a frame of mind which is close to that of prayer."
– Henri Matisse

Matisse claimed to know God
Only when he was at work
(Matisse that is
Or was it God?)
He found him
Indecipherable
(Matisse or God?)
On the torn territory
Of his imagination
(this must be Matisse)
Were splashed
Improvisations
That he suspected
Of being
No more than
Divine conjuring-tricks.

Lord, come conjure

IV

MALIGNANT SADNESS

What is depression? The black dog.
Depleted serotonin in the brain.
Not seeing the point of deciding
                on the smallest thing.
Toughened glass
                between the soul and joy.
And every day
                adds a layer to the glass.

What is recovery? Unexpected hopefulness.
Restored balance of transmitters.
Surprisingly deciding
                to trust again.
Seeing meltwater
                roll across a frozen pond
And every day
                thin more ice to transparency.

The title is from a book by the scientist Lewis Wolpert on his own depression.

ACCOMPANYING MALIGNANT SADNESS

I am an attendant lord
to your deep sorrow. At first
I nagged, cajoled, sought to subvert.
Then I managed, arranged,
sent word across the satrapies.

Power proves empty before helplessness
in the one loved. At your audiences
with caring professionals
I am available in an alcove
should I be required.

Life at court turns
dowager-quiet, over the old silver
and my cut-glass longing.
Sometimes your eyes catch light
gone before I can speak it.

At night I comfort you,
dream of revolution.
I dread the day
I am in receipt of *lettres de cachet*
detaining you in a place of safety.

DECEMBER JAY
  for S.

When I see you in our wood
you are a splendid crazy flash of blue
accompanying your flight
with a raucous protest-call.

In these days,
either side of the winter solstice,
a different jay can be seen, fifteen feet
from my writing-desk.

The bird that annexed the wood
with colour and loud courage
stands under the feeder, picking
discards from the mud.

The feathers on your head are short and spare.
They give you the look
of one who has seen too much pain.
I can only just see the furled blue.

I know it is there, beyond these lightless days,
wit and electricity, blaze
of laughter and pride and protest.
I know it is there.

PASTORAL ENCOURAGEMENT FROM THE LATEST EXOPLANET RESEARCH

Last night the Russians were shelling a nuclear power plant
but we did not stare, through endless darkness,
at clouds of iron and corundum.

Since lockdown, some days seem to lack all purpose, nothing
                                              to be done but hide.
At least water molecules are not ripped apart above us
for their atoms to be blown round the planet at Mach 14.

The latest climate news is bad, then always worse,
but when we journey on the dark side, my suffering love and I,
we endure no onslaught of titanium rain.

Reference: "Diurnal variations in the stratosphere of the ultrahot giant exoplanet WASP-121b" by Thomas Mikal-Evans, David K. Sing, Joanna K. Barstow, Tiffany Kataria, Jayesh Goyal, Nikole Lewis, Jake Taylor, Nathan J. Mayne, Tansu Daylan, Hannah R. Wakeford, Mark S. Marley and Jessica J. Spake, 21 February 2022, *Nature Astronomy*.

GOLDFINCHES

I measure out an aliquot of fine black seed.
Each is oval, slightly pointed. They fall like black rain
Into the feeder. They are a lure
To get our goldfinches back.

Our lives have lacked those fine flashes of wing,
Those self-satisfied cardinals' heads.
My hopes, these days, are no bigger
Than nyger seeds. I do not tell you that.

They slip with a drenching whisper
They feel as though they could fall
Through fine mesh, and be lost altogether.
Somehow they stay in place.

I do not pour too many, lest they rot.
I do not tell you that.
I kiss the sleeping head that might still dream
Charms of goldfinches into my grim heart.

SWIFTS

Watched over the Lyon river
On our honeymoon
Watched around the Galata Tower in Istanbul
And in their hurtling dance
Here at Carcassonne, against this film-set
Of Visigothic towers that interrupt
The sun.
        Swifts have been mascots
Of our love, and like our love
Fly with one half of their brains
Even when the other half sleeps.
          And they are always looking, looking
For next prey, as we have looked hungrily
For the world.
       One day
Swifts will roost and close their wings
Let it not be soon.

V

LEXICON

Leather-bound, not of the first quality.
Institutional brown leather of 1889.
'Ramsgate Centre', embossed in gold.
Mine is a childhood in a family that wonders,
breaks off conversations
                           to hunt in reference books.
And this is the most special,
because it is the heaviest, and thus
a particular honour for the child
deputed to fetch it.
                     And what is more
although my father talks the most
(and must not be contradicted)
this book is one that
                           only my mother can read.

In it we look up Homeric words for tears,
Plato's for the transmigration of souls.
We dwell on excellence (my father
tells me I do not possess this). My mother
keeps her silent counsel, communes
with the strange script, the Ramsgate Centre,
a line of wonder stretching
                           to Socrates and beyond.
Twenty years after her death
I am still searching between the leather-covered boards
for tears, souls, excellences.

FRESHMAN

I am absolutely full of my new adventure.
It begins tonight. Three years of parties and punting
And being taught by Nobel Prizewinners.
My fifty-year-old mother has driven me here, helped me unpack.
She is absurdly old, but always useful.

After some ethnic dinner or other
Which I can hardly choke down for excitement
We walk back to my glass-and-concrete room
(The building has won a major award)
Then over to her car. When she is gone

I feel curiously lost, and take refuge
In staring at College noticeboards
Which mean nothing to me at all.
These are the days
Before student induction has been invented.

My mother, who in my view is almost too old
To be allowed on the road by herself
Embarks on a nocturnal exploration of the fen country,
Driving fast, taking roads at random,
Dreaming of Peter Wimsey.

When I turn fifty I am still replaying
The mistakes and blunders
Of those years, and trying to teach the young
To make a few less. My mother has just died,
My best friend in all the world.

All my life she did her utmost to teach me
There is always another adventure.

ANTONIA

Her name is Antonia, or Karen, or Zoe.
She speaks to me of shabby, intense interiors –
wind-chimes, aniline lamps, royal yashmuks
someone brought back from somewhere.

I am welcomed, or at least accepted,
though I am not the someone from far away
but the same familiar local need
for reassurance, and just to be noticed.

I have not read *The Golden Notebook*, but
have ticked Faulkner, Fitzgerald, Hermann Hesse,
and made my choices –
for Shelley over Keats, Eliot over Yeats.

I recite my opinions. I memorise
how her body looks in repose, how
she flicks her hips when she dances
how she laughs at my shyness.

We are only riding the Circle Line
debating when to change. We share
one extraordinary kiss, when we are both
with other people, and making other plans.

And one day she is gone, to Shetland or Düsseldorf,
or Santa Fe. She sends me postcards
of cubist nudes, staircases by MC Escher, unreadable texts
of what might have been, abandon, abandoned.

SCRATCHES

After sex
I place five pebbles
on your naked back.

I can no more keep
this moment
than fly to the moon.

The Japanese love not
the first exuberance
of cherry blossom

but the moment
when a faint breeze
gives it weightless fall.

You wake
and tell me your new fellowship
is on the far side of the moon.

Pebbles
thrown hard and flat
score scratches in new asphalt.

A POEM OF LOVE AND ENVY

A quiet room
full of quiet, good choices.
Pots glazed in muted colours.
A close-up of the grain of boulders.
The view over the loch
                 to Torridon.
I like to picture you there
at the writing-desk
or wrestling
with Mozart's scoring for clarinet.

I always imagined myself
contriving such a purposeful space
and buy endless box files
not making it happen.

Grace and peace remain elusive
but at least I hear now
over the ground bass of my disorder
                 a clarinet line
wry and playful and wistful by turns
and compose in my head

letters unsent from a writing-desk.

SEEN ON A T-SHIRT

Seen on a t-shirt
Champagne should be
    Dry
        Cold
            And Free.

Wisdom in threes? Let's try it.

Steak should be
    Rib-eye
        Chargrilled
            And very rare.

Ice-cream should be
    Fresh
        Home-made
            And peach, or pistachio, or passion-fruit.

What about work?

Colleagues should be
    Diverse
        Energetic
            And crazy enough to want to work with me.

Under the t-shirt?

Lovemaking should be
    Naked
        Eyes wide, heart open.
            And always surprising.

The shirt, once back on, should be
>   Tight
>> Bright red
>>> Or crushed water-melon.

Friendship should be
> So new as to be full of strangeness
>> Or so long-standing
>>> As to need nothing explained.

Grief should be
> Itself
>> Fiercely-spoken, quietly sung,
>>> And take as long as it takes.

And joy?

Joy should be
> Poured carefully
>> Into a tilted glass
>>> And savoured with the one person in the world
>>> Who really understands you.

THE PEARL EARRING
(from the painting by Vermeer)

I was not some whore
paid to counterfeit innocence,
some daughter decency forgot.

I was respectable, in need of no adventure,
mesmerised by his laugh, the way he looked at light,
his craft of living, his love of making work.

Even by the way he hesitated
to take what I couldn't refuse him.
He taught me the art of waiting

and how love can give itself away
in an over-shoulder look.

KEATS'S STAR

From his window he can see the setting moon
And to the south the jewel-like light
Of Venus. This may be his final poem,
His last gaze across the Spanish Stair. He might,
If it were only in God's gift, freeze
This moment, shine without pain like that pearl
In the Roman sky, or be one with this breeze
Off the sea, freed from all his fear.

Early sun slides across the marble steps. He knows
He will climb them again only in a pine box.
He thinks of his lover in black, one red rose
Clutched for all their struggle, spirits in paradox.
If only his lips could meet between her breasts
On that star-shaped mole. One last kiss.

HOPKINS ON SYMI

> *Gerard Manley Hopkins, a Jesuit priest and lifelong celibate, lecturing on Helen of Troy, suddenly broke off and told his students "You know, I never saw a woman naked. I wish I had."*
> – quotation from Paul Mariani, *Gerard Manley Hopkins: A Life* (New York: Viking, 2008), p. 391.

I place Hopkins at the harbour on Symi
One bright-hot Aegean day, toward evening.
There he sees bellbright Hellenic boys
No older than ten, howling with laughter
As they play in the light-showered waves.

They know their Hopkins, and perform
Downdolphinry which is the same in every language,
Running round onto the quay to jump, knees clasped,
Into the glittering water, then splash out,
Naked as jaybirds, to chase each other to the next jump.

But it is not for them that I have brought
Inscape's great lover all this way.
It is for the girl at the end of the quay,
Tall, slim, wearing nothing but a bikini bottom,
She contemplates the bay, knowing herself stared at.

I let him look long upon her, in profile.
Her breasts are like young roes.
She is beautiful as Tirzah, comely as Jerusalem,
Terrible as an army with banners.
For once in his life, he allows himself to look.

At once he makes her into myth.
Here is Calypso, awaiting Odysseus,
Here is Eve, gazing back at Eden.
I send him to meet her, angular in his black soutane
(faded now, and shiny from over-wear),

He speaks to her courteously.
They talk of Sappho, Alcaeus.
He searches for the longing in her soul.
He offers to hear her confession.
His lectures on Helen of Troy are greatly improved.

VI

EULOGY AT THE MEMORIAL SERVICE FOR A GLACIER

What shall we want to hold in our hearts about you?
From a distance, the way you roamed corries

caressing outcrops, the way you shone
in the least fleeting sunlight.

Closer to, the corrugated mystery of your surface
always different from day to day.

Your paradoxes: that such beauty could scour ground
leaching water full of toxic rock;

that you were made of life-giving water
and killed whatever animal was stranded on you.

Your resurrection will await the next ice age –
hard to imagine we shall keep you company then.

DEBATE ON A PANDEMIC

Our theorists disagree
            as to whether the term trauma
is properly applied to this crisis.
            It has been of slow onset
so perhaps better seen
            as a complex pattern of loss.

So we monitor
            grief reactions across the whole community.
And we debate hope
            for some still think
this will stabilise
            that the infecting agent

will learn to live with us.
            Others point to past invasions
to show that its killing sprees
            never stabilise.
Look, they say, at the time
            it crossed the Bering Strait.

We lost then
            three quarters of large land animals.
This is telling, certainly,
            and the hotheaded ravens
go on to insist on complete removal
            as the only long-term solution.

Perhaps what we are not allowed to call trauma
                has made me weak
but I still demur
                and argue in the Council of All Beings
spreading my old bat-wings wide
                this time, this time, send a warning.

'THE FIGHTING TEMERAIRE, TUGGED TO HER LAST BERTH TO BE BROKEN UP, 1838'
from the painting by J.M.W. Turner

The past had endured
what the present does not even dream of.

The present is round-bottomed,
cylindrical, efficient. It hauls
the past away, having computed its costs.

The reflections of the past
in the timeless river
draw the eye all the way to depth.

The sun sets in heedless magnificence
reducing the present to the faintest of lines.

TWO STUDIES FROM T.S. ELIOT'S 'JOURNEY OF THE MAGI'

Self-appraisal of a mage

Principal achievement during the appraisal period?
                                    Difficult journey in winter.

Punctuality?
                                    Just in time.

Main difficulties experienced?
                                    Lazy and corrupt camel-drivers.

Disappointments?
                                    Not enough sherbet.

Self-assessment of performance?
                                    Satisfactory.

Best relationship with work colleague?
                                    Balthasar, balm to my soul.

Most problematic relationship?
                                    Melchior. Argues back.

Information provided for the furtherance of your work?
                                    None.

Future developmental aspirations?
                                    Being part of a death.

Such a long journey

We had a theory. It meant travelling westward.
At first, simple enough. We each had resources.
We lost most of them on the Straits of Hormuz;
our boatman betrayed us to pirates.
Perhaps that was the moment to turn back
after we'd bargained our release for gold and incense
leaving only a few coins sewn into an old hat.
But we had come so far
                        and a theory
can become a story you would wander the world to tell.

We were in trouble, sometimes, misunderstood,
always there for each other – always walking westward,
taken on by an Ethiopian eunuch, even though by then
only one of us was fit to work – slipping away
by night when we sensed we were near.
He was a philosopher and carried his own coffin;
we raided it for myrrh. Took millings
from the edge of one of his ingots,
saved a last joss-stick. We had read our Isaiah.
And we had a theory

that at some place under a setting star
three gifts could be exchanged for peace
passing all understanding. What we ended up giving
were some much-needed hints on run-routes
for a family of refugees.

BOWLING GREEN MARSH, TOPSHAM

Mudflats like the skinned hide
of a great dead animal, and the river
bloodless wash winding across the carcass.

A lone egret subjects the liverish mud
to expert attention. A stabbing beak
confirms his results. Dunlin in a wide flock

rise like a flung-out scarf
drift down onto a different flat.

Further out, the Exe has caught the low sun.
It sweeps the serpent of the Clyst
out to the distant sea.

In a locked-down winter
I do not raise my gaze
to this far light.

Slow washing of dead flats, and a solitary egret
compel the eye.

DEER, TOWARD DUSK

Steep field, almost dusk.
Over the woods, fading view
to everywhere. At the sound of the gate-latch
deer, mid-field, startle, attend.
Sentries are vigilant. For a full minute
we are all content to look.
As I inch into the slope
they fidget, and then as though
a single movement of spirit had run
through them all in the same moment
set off in fluid canter
for the far hedge.

My eyes devour the sweetness of their running.

In a dip, perched on his haunches,
the redness of a dog-fox.
He stares them down. Even in this light
his eyes glitter predator.
He is a tenth of their size
but a million years of wolves
shock their collective amygdala.
They double back, across, upward, anywhere away,
my suspicious hat forgotten,
and are gone, vaulting an impossible bank.
All our hormones subside.
The fox and I are alone. Night seeps in.

BETTER WORLDS

Better World Books, from Dunfermline,
supply me with a copy
of the poems of Szymborska.
'Dark, complex, and profoundly intelligent'
according to *The Washington Post*.

The book is from the Lucan Library.
A label on the back cover
is stamped 'withdrawn from stock'.

Now I know this is none other
than the gate of the barbarians.
Even the Nobel Prize for Literature
is not enough
to keep one's book in a library.

A strange and wicked consolation
to those poets
unrecognised by *The Washington Post*.

I am thinking of looking
in Better World Books, Cracow branch,
for a copy of Lord Lucan.
Dark and complex, even by the standards
of the profoundly intelligent Szymborska.

Murdered the nanny,
vanished without trace,
guaranteed his fame.

RABBIT HOLE

> *Lewis Carroll's father was a canon at Ripon Cathedral. The son often worshipped there, and one of the carvings has been identified as a source for his writing.*

The end of evensong on the twenty-first Sunday.
Through moted, ecclesiastical light
as the choir departs, solemn and mock-solemn,
a canon's son discerns a faint smile
                            broad as a roof-boss
with whiskers at its edges.

He remains in an attitude of prayer
(thereby fending off
assertive verger
and curious prebend)
making friends with the Cat in the air

finally he slides from his stall,
sees a rabbit hurtling for its carved burrow,
taloned gryphon in pursuit,
and hears his father
tutting at his pocket-watch. "We'll be late.
She'll have our heads."

The son bows to the Cat,
thinks of Miss Liddell,
mutters an apology about polynomials.
Nothing is in his head
                        but falling.

LADIES WHO TREK

Two grey-haired ladies on the train.
Seventy, perhaps. They are strangers.
Slightly deaf. Slightly loud.
One asks the other about her book
On the Silk Road.
             Lady B explains
She is in the process of walking
Across North-West China.
             Ah yes,
Lady A knows that part of the world.
Fascinating area.
             Lady B explains
She can't do the high mountains any more,
Since that time she passed out on the glacier field.
Lady A asks where the jeep will drop her
For her trek.
             North-East Pakistan –
Not so dangerous now as the North-West.
Lady A nods, and fetches down her bag.

And off they go,
Ever so slightly competitive
Swopping titles on the history of indigo
Striding across the glacier fields of Paddington
Refusing to believe they will pass out.

PARTHENON IN SUNLIGHT, GATEWAY IN SHADOW

I have walked the path of those shadows
with my mother. I remember
the quality of the marble, abraded
by many million feet, the exact
placement of every pedestal.

The photograph was hers.
She bought it in Cambridge
from the Heffer Gallery, Sidney St,
in her student days, pursuing
excellence, and truth in beauty.

The picture-cord has rotted
and our wild kitten has pulled the print
off the wall. The glass is not broken;
framed in ordinary wartime wood
Attic sunlight still gleams out of shadow.

I turn over the old frame
with its peeling backing and its faded label.
My mother is twenty years dead.
I am left to hold the truth
of the wild kitten and the rotted cord

the feel of worn Pentelic marble
underfoot, and the lie of ancient sunshine.

PETROGLYPHS, ARIZONA

There is a dream dreaming us.
Sometimes the dream
Says ladder. I know
Those times, their longings,
Their feeling of almost.

Sometimes the dream
Says lizard. It says
Bask in the sunlight
But be ready to sprint for cover
Under the nearest stone.

Sometimes the dream
Says rattlesnake. I know this too
But I am never ready
For the speed of disaster
Venom's draining of hope.

I am still the young brave
Being led to the ceremony
To learn the dream.
I am the bitter elder
Watching from the broken ladder

Eyes, lidless, studying the stone.

The first line is a statement made by a member of the San people to the explorer Laurens van der Post.

A PLACE FOR POETRY

A high light room. Long windows look
Down a heathered hillside to a waterfall.
Behind my chair, tall shelves house every book
On which I might conceivably want to call.
On either side wall, big bevelled mirrors
Reflect books, view, books again.
This is a place lacking all terrors –
Absent listlessness, sorrow, self-disdain.
I write in the mornings, in fountain pen,
Interrupted only by my wife bringing tea,
Or a little silver cat, demanding to know when
I have ever seen anyone as beautiful as she.
At evening, nurtured by much candlelight,
I watch falling water fade into night.